THE NILE

written and photographed by

Julia Waterlow

RSVP

RAINTREE
STECK-VAUGHN
P U B L I S H E R S
The Steck-Vaughn Company

Austin, Texas

*Cover: Feluccas, the traditional Nile boats,
on the river at Aswan*

Series and book editor: Rosemary Ashley
Series designer: Derek Lee
Cover design: Scott Melcer

Library of Congress Cataloging-in-Publishing Data
Waterlow, Julia.
     The Nile / written and photographed by Julia Waterlow.
        p.   cm. — (Rivers of the world)
     Includes bibliographical references and index.
     Summary: Describes the course of the Nile River from its
source in central Africa to the Mediterranean Sea and people
who have explored it, civilizations it has fostered, efforts to
control it, and more.
     ISBN 0–8114–3100–2
     1. Nile River Valley—Juvenile literature.   2. Nile River—
Juvenile literature.   [1. Nile River.   2. Nile River Valley.]
I. Series: Rivers of the world (Austin, Tex.)
DT115.W34   1994   92-39951
962—dc20   CIP
                                                       AC

Typeset by Multifacit Graphics, Keyport, NJ
Printed in Italy by G. Canale C.S.p.A.
Bound in the United States by Lake Book, Melrose Park, IL
1 2 3 4 5 6 7 8 9 0 LB 99 98 97 96 95 94

RIVERS OF THE WORLD

The Amazon
The Ganges
The Mississippi
The Nile
The Rhine
The Thames

CONTENTS

1
River of Life

Looking at a map, you can see why the ancient Egyptians thought the Nile River was like a flower: its long stem curves north through the African desert and finally blossoms in a fan-shaped spread of water channels as it reaches the Mediterranean Sea. But the Egyptians were never able to discover where the "roots" of their river lay. Now we know that the Nile rises far to the south, on the equator. It is the longest river in the world, flowing a distance of 4,160 miles, about as far as the distance from New York to London.

Today, as throughout history, the people of the Lower Nile would be helpless without the river. So little rain falls in this northern part of Africa that if there were no Nile, there would be no water and nothing could grow. Lining either side of the river is a green ribbon of vegetation where people grow their crops; beyond lies barren desert.

For over five thousand years there has been civilization along the Nile, making it one of the oldest occupied places on Earth. Throughout history, the people of the Nile Valley have been measuring and recording water levels because their lives depended on the river. No other river has been studied so carefully over such a long time period.

For just as long, people have been trying to control the river. Building canals, embankments, basins, and barrages has always been part of life beside the Nile. In the last hundred years, new technology has led to the invention of bigger controls with much greater effects. Projects like the huge Aswan Dam have changed the river, its valley, and people's lives more than anything else in the last few thousand years. Big dam and irrigation projects provide benefits, but cause problems too, some of which are difficult to solve.

The lush green Nile Valley has been farmed for centuries.

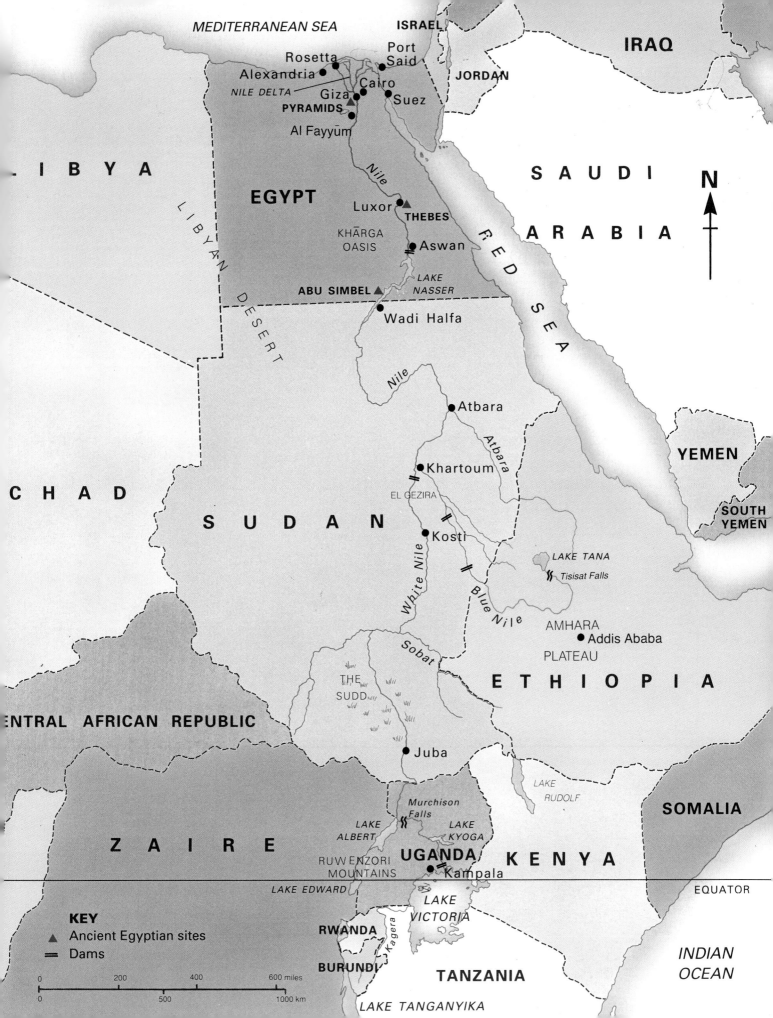

MEDITERRANEAN SEA

ISRAEL

IRAQ

Rosetta
Port
Said
Alexandria
JORDAN
Cairo
NILE DELTA
Giza
Suez
PYRAMIDS
Al Fayyūm

LIBYA

EGYPT

SAUDI

Nile

Luxor
THEBES

ARABIA

N

KHĀRGA
OASIS

Aswan

RED

ABU SIMBEL

LAKE
NASSER

Wadi Halfa

SEA

Nile

CHAD

Atbara

YEMEN

Khartoum

Atbara

SOUTH
YEMEN

SUDAN

EL GEZIRA

LAKE TANA

Kosti

Tisisat Falls

White Nile

Blue Nile

AMHARA

Sobat

Addis Ababa

ENTRAL AFRICAN REPUBLIC

PLATEAU

THE
SUDD

ETHIOPIA

Juba

LAKE
RUDOLF

ZAIRE

Murchison
Falls

SOMALIA

LAKE
ALBERT

LAKE
KYOGA

RUWENZORI
MOUNTAINS

UGANDA

KENYA

Kampala

EQUATOR

LAKE EDWARD

Kagera

LAKE
VICTORIA

KEY
▲ Ancient Egyptian sites
═ Dams

INDIAN
OCEAN

RWANDA

BURUNDI

TANZANIA

0   200   400   600 miles
0   500   1000 km

LAKE TANGANYIKA

2
From Source to Sea

The Upper Nile

Far south on the equator, in the middle of Africa, mountains covered in snow and ice rise from the plains. These are the Ruwenzori Mountains on the borders of Uganda and Zaire. Also called the Mountains of the Moon, the highest peaks reach 17,075 feet. From this point streams run down and feed a huge lake, Lake Victoria. Each stream can claim to be a source of the Nile, but the great river's real journey begins where it pours north out of Lake Victoria, in Uganda.

There are many lakes and waterfalls in this area. Leaving Lake Victoria, the Nile once cascaded down the Ripon Falls (these are now covered by a reservoir behind a dam). After passing through marshy Lake Kyoga, the young Nile roars over the Murchison Falls, dropping about 130 feet. Even after the next great lake, Lake Albert, the Nile continues to churn up white water as it meets a series of rapids farther downstream.

Lying almost on the equator, the area surrounding the Upper Nile is always wet (with an average of 50 inches of

The Nile flows north for thousands of miles from Lake Victoria, a huge lake bordering several countries on the equator.

Hippopotamuses love to wallow in the waters of the Upper Nile.

rainfall per year) and, except high in the mountains, very warm. The vegetation is lush and tropical. There is plenty of wildlife, too. Elephants, lions, rhinoceros, buffalo, and antelope can be seen in game reserves like the Murchison Falls National Park. The lakes and the river are teeming with many types of fish. The river is also home to the wallowing hippopotamus and the basking crocodile.

Not long after entering the Sudan, the Nile begins to slow down and spread out over flat land. The river has reached the Sudd, an Arabic word which means "obstacle." The Sudd is certainly an obstacle: It is the biggest area of swamp in the world, stretching about 435 miles

Source of the Nile

Although the main Nile River starts where it pours out of Lake Victoria, its source lies farther south. Of the many streams that flow into Lake Victoria, the largest is called the Kagera River. It begins near Lake Tanganyika and is said to be the true source of the Nile.

Storks and many other birds make their home in the vast swamps of the Sudd.

from south to north. This vast marshy area is a maze of thick papyrus reeds and grasses. The Nile zigzags through the swamp in channels that constantly change as plants grow over them. Huge grass islands floating in the water are almost firm enough to hold elephants. It is hot here and very wet in the rainy season. There is too much water for large land animals, but it is a paradise for many types of water birds, including herons, storks, and pelicans.

Although there is so much water flowing into the Sudd, large amounts are continually being lost by evaporation. The Nile River that finally finds its way out of the swamp only carries about one-seventh of all the water that reaches Egypt. The rest of the Nile's water is carried in streams and smaller rivers called tributaries that join the Nile north of the Sudd. Most of these tributaries come from the Ethiopian mountains, to the east.

Papyrus

The ancient Egyptians invented writing and a kind of paper called papyrus. This was made from a plant called papyrus, which is a reed that grew in many places on the edge of the Nile. The stem was thinly sliced and strips were pressed together and beaten. Then they were left to dry between two stones.

Our word ''paper'' comes from the word papyrus. A kind of picture writing, called hieroglyphics, was used by the ancient Egyptians to record events on their papyrus paper.

A passenger ferry crosses the Blue Nile in the Sudan.

The tributaries

The river flowing from Lake Victoria is known as the White Nile; about halfway to the sea it is joined by its most important tributary, the Blue Nile. The Blue Nile is much shorter than the White Nile, but it is important because it carries more water. The two other main Nile tributaries, the Sobat and the At-

bara, also carry much of the water that feeds the Nile. In an average year the Blue Nile supplies fifty-nine percent, the Sobat fourteen percent, the Atbara thirteen percent, and the White Nile only fourteen percent of all the water that finally reaches Egypt.

All these rivers have high and low seasons. At certain times of the year there is particularly heavy rainfall in

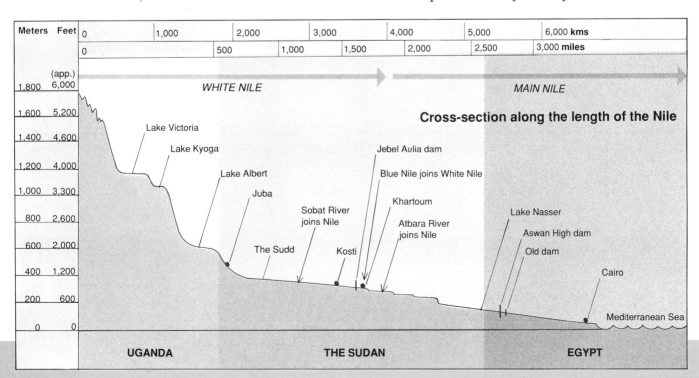

Cross-section along the length of the Nile

the mountainous areas that feed the rivers and they swell to several times their normal size. At its peak in August and September, the Blue Nile provides 95 percent of the total Nile water. Its effect is rather like a tidal wave rushing downstream.

The Blue Nile begins its journey at Lake Tana in Ethiopia. Shortly after leaving the lake, it plunges over the Tisisat Falls. It then crashes and tumbles for half its course through a gorge cut deep in the mountains, the sides are nearly 4,925 feet high in places. It is not until the Blue Nile reaches the plains of the Sudan that it begins to slow down.

North of the Sudd in the Sudan, the land around the Nile becomes drier. The vegetation is often just thorny scrub and long grasses. There are two seasons, the wet and the dry. When the rains come in the summer, the heat and dust of the dry season give way to sprouting green shoots.

Where the Blue Nile meets the White Nile at Khartoum, the two rivers flow side by side for several miles, not mixing. You can see the different colors clearly. The White Nile is actually brownish-gray from the silt it has picked up along its way and the Blue Nile is clearer and greenish-blue. But when the Blue Nile is in full flood, it too becomes cloudy with the thousands of tons of silt it has scoured out of the Ethiopian mountains.

On the entire 1,860 mile stretch from Khartoum to the Mediterranean Sea,

An aerial view of the Nile basin and tributary rivers in southern Sudan.

Lake Nasser is the biggest human-made lake in the world. It was formed when the Egyptians built the Aswan Dam.

only one more river, the Atbara, joins the Nile. This means that unlike most rivers, the Nile does not get wider as it nears the sea. After Khartoum, the river is broken up by a series of rapids, known as the Nile cataracts. The water spills and churns over hard rocks sticking out of the riverbed, making it difficult for boats to travel in these areas.

As the Nile reaches the border of the Sudan and Egypt, it flows into the biggest human-made lake in the world, Lake Nasser. The lake is more than 310 miles long. It was formed when the Nile was blocked off by the building of the Aswan Dam (1960–1970). The flow of the Nile beyond the dam is now totally under human control.

The fertile valley

North of Aswan, the Nile travels more slowly. To the west of the river lies the Libyan desert (the Sahara) and to the east, the Arabian desert. So little rain falls in the lower Nile Valley (less than half an inch per year) that people can build their houses of mud bricks knowing that there is little chance of their homes being washed away.

Even though there is desert all around, the Nile Valley is at its most fertile here. Before the Aswan Dam was built the Nile would overflow its banks every year and flood the surrounding valley. As the flood water subsided, rich sediment would be left behind. This made fertile soil and, with plenty of water from the Nile, crops grew well. Today, land varying in width from a few feet to about 30 miles is still cultivated on both sides of the Nile.

This part of the Nile valley is so heavily populated that much of the wildlife has disappeared. Fish and birds are still seen in and around the river. However, the much larger animals like crocodiles and hippopotamuses have been hunted to extinction.

The Delta

The Nile reaches the last stage in its life as it nears the sea. The ground slopes so gently that the river flows very slowly.

The Nile can no longer carry its remaining load of silt, and so some is washed away by the sea and the rest is left behind. The river finds a way through this silt and splits into several channels, spreading the sediment into a fan shape. Water collects in marshes, often enclosed by spits of sand shaped by the sea.

This whole area is called a river's delta. The Nile Delta was formed in this way over thousands of years. It now has two main branches running to the sea but most of the water in the delta is carefully controlled in canals. Since the building of the Aswan Dam, sediment is no longer carried down and deposited by the river and the delta is gradually being eroded by the sea.

Here is the mouth of the Nile near Rosetta. Just north of Cairo the river splits into several channels which run out to meet the sea at different places along the coast.

3
Countries and People of the Nile

The Nile rises in Uganda and passes through the Sudan where the Blue Nile joins it from Ethiopia. The river finishes its journey in Egypt. Of all these countries, Egypt is the most modern and advanced. The others have suffered recently from civil wars and droughts, leaving them poor and struggling to rebuild their economies.

"Egypt, the gift of the Nile"

Toward the end of the great ancient Egyptian civilization (which lasted from about 3000–30 B.C.), Egypt was invaded by many different conquering peoples, including the Greeks and the Romans. But it was the Arab conquest (A.D. 639–42) that has left the most lasting effect.

An Egyptian farmer and his family in the courtyard of their mud-built house. Families in Egypt are often large and the population is growing rapidly.

The people grow vegetables near their houses in an Egyptian village.

Today Arabic is the official language and Islam the official religion in both Egypt and the Sudan. Egyptians usually say their country is part of the Middle East rather than Africa.

Egypt is almost totally dependent on the waters of the Nile; in fact there is probably no other country in the world that needs a river so much in order to survive. Although Egypt is a large country, more than three times the size of Arizona, less than five percent of the land is fit to live on because most is desert. Apart from a few oases, nearly all the fertile land is beside the river, and this is where the people live.

In the far south of Egypt and spreading into the Sudan is a different race of people, the Nubians. They have lived along this part of the Nile for as long as anyone can discover. Although of African origin, they have mixed with the Arabs and adopted Islam as their religion. Much of their ancient kingdom of Nubia lay where Lake Nasser is today and thousands of Nubians lost their homes when the Aswan Dam was built.

The peoples of the Sudan

The middle section of the Nile runs through the Sudan, the largest country in Africa, more than twice the size of Egypt. For thousands of years Egyptians and Arabs raided the Sudan for slaves. Arabs began to settle in the Sudan,

Muslims pray in a Cairo mosque. Most Egyptians and many Sudanese are Muslim.

14

Wild camels are brought to be sold in a camel market near Aswan.

particularly in the north, and inter-married with local people. The Arabic people of the Sudan are the majority and they control the government.

Away from the north and the capital, Khartoum, the Sudan's people are very different. Nearly all are Africans, belonging to tribal groups. There are hundreds of tribes. Three of the main tribes, living in the south near the Nile, are the Dinka, the Nuer, and the Shilluk. They are very tall, lean people, many of whom live by cattle herding. They scar their faces with their own tribal patterns. Like many tribal southern Sudanese, they believe in spirit gods and not in the Islamic religion. This is one of the reasons for the civil war which is now being fought between the peoples in the north and the south of the Sudan.

Away from the green valley watered by the Nile lies barren desert.

Shahad, a Potter

"These pots are drying out. I make them from clay that I dig up beside the river. When I have made a big batch of pots, I pack them on a cart with straw. My donkey pulls the load to the nearest town where I sell them. The big pots are traditional water jars that we use at home to keep our water in. Not many people in the countryside have taps in their houses. Women use a different type of clay pot to collect drinking water from wells—they balance the pots on their heads."

Uganda

South of the Sudan, in Uganda, the people are Bantu. Uganda was colonized by the British and given independence in 1962. Trouble started in 1971 when a man named Idi Amin took power and killed many people who opposed him. Now life is returning to normal. Farmers do not need to rely on the Nile's water in Uganda because there is so much rain, but, near Lake Victoria, the Nile is used to make hydroelectricity at the Owen Falls Dam.

Ethiopia

The source of the Blue Nile lies in a very ancient African kingdom, Ethiopia. Much of the country lies high up in mountains and the Nile is almost impossible to reach here because it flows through such a steep gorge. Ethiopia is one of the few African countries not to have been conquered by outsiders or colonized by Europeans for any length of time. It was also one of the first countries in the world to become Christian. Today it is trying to recover after years of civil war and famine.

This woman belongs to the Dinka tribe. Her face is scarred with the tribal markings typical of the Dinka people.

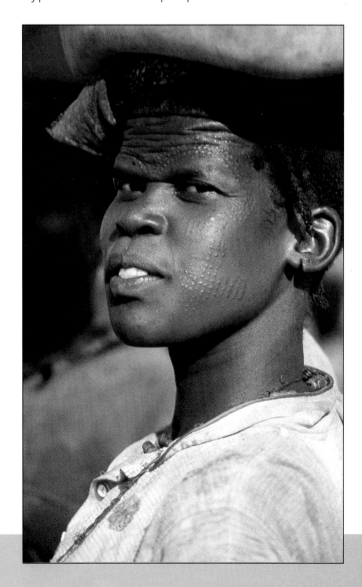

4
Ancient Civilizations of the Nile

Over thousands of years the Nile carried vast amounts of fertile soil and silt into the land we now call Egypt. With its warm climate and well-watered valley, crops could be grown easily. It is not surprising that one of the world's oldest and greatest civilizations flourished in this lush region of the Nile and its valley.

Before 3000 B.C. there were two kingdoms lying along the banks of the Lower Nile. A king named Menes united them into one great state, Egypt. For the next three thousand years, pharaohs (the name given to ancient Egyptian kings)

An ancient picture of the Nile Delta shows people hunting and fishing among the marshes.

Above The Great Pyramid was built for Cheops, whose reign began about 2589 B.C. The Sphinx is named after a mythical Greek monster with a human's head and lion's body.

Opposite This temple at Dandara is dedicated to Hathor, the Egyptian goddess of pleasure. At the top of each column is a carved head of Hathor.

ruled the land beside the Nile. One of the pharaoh's most important jobs was the care of the river.

In the late summer, the Nile would flood. If the flood was too low it would not water the land, crops would not grow, and people would starve; if the floods rose too high, villages and fields might be washed away. Because they depended so much on the river, the ancient Egyptians had to learn about and control the water that flowed through their land. They dug canals and made small dams, and began to measure the Nile's rise and fall. They invented a 365-day calendar, based on the river's

changes throughout the year. To calculate the size of fields, they worked out a system of measurement, geometry.

The mathematics and engineering they learned from studying the Nile helped the ancient Egyptians become great builders of their times. The most famous monuments they have left are the pyramids. The pyramids were built as tombs for the pharaohs. Inside, the pyramid burial chamber was filled with jewelry, food, and furniture because the ancient Egyptians believed in life after death. They wanted the dead king to have as much comfort and luxury as when he was alive.

Ramses II, the warrior pharaoh, liked to build massive temples to impress his people.

The pyramids were built during the Old Kingdom, which lasted until 2258 B.C. During the next great period of Egyptian history, the Middle Kingdom, the capital was moved from Memphis, near Cairo, up the Nile to Thebes, now called Luxor.

The ancient Egyptians believed in hundreds of gods, two of the most important being the Sun and the Nile River. Temples were constructed all along the river and in the delta, and tombs were built into hillsides above the flood plain. Prayers and even sacrifices were made to the Nile in the hope that this would please the river god and the annual flood would bring a good harvest.

Perhaps the greatest period of ancient Egyptian civilization was the New Kingdom which began in 1570 B.C. The Egyptian empire spread up the Nile valley and beyond. The population of

The Pyramid of Cheops

The Pyramid of Cheops is the northernmost and oldest pyramid at Giza, near Cairo. It is built of stone blocks weighing 2.5 tons each. In 2600 B.C. the Egyptians had no machines to help them and each block had to be dragged into place. It is a masterpiece of engineering. It took 100,000 men twenty years to build the pyramid. The French emperor, Napoleon, who invaded Egypt in 1798, estimated that there were enough stones in the three pyramids at Giza to build a wall 10 feet high all around France.

Main Dates in the History of the Nile B.C.

3100 B.C.—Kingdoms along the Nile in Egypt united by King Menes.

3110–2258 B.C.—Old Kingdom in Egypt. They begin to study and measure the Nile. The pyramids are built.

2000–1786 B.C.—Middle Kingdom.

1570–1085 B.C.—New Kingdom. Great tombs built across the Nile from the capital, Thebes.

1085–322 B.C.—Late Period. Egypt has many rulers. Persians and other peoples invade the country.

322–30 B.C.—Ptolemaic Period. Alexander the Great invades Egypt. The Greek general, Ptolemy, becomes pharaoh (Ptolemy I), adopts the Egyptian gods, and builds many temples.

30 B.C.—the Romans conquer Egypt.

Thebes grew to more than one million. Huge statues, monuments, and tombs were built for the pharaohs and their nobles. On the east bank of the Nile lay the city; on the west bank were the tombs for the dead. The Nile itself was Egypt's highway. Wheeled vehicles were never needed because the people had boats and the river.

In 1344 B.C. a young pharaoh named Tutankhamen died. Like all other dead pharaohs he was embalmed and put in a magnificent painted tomb in a desert valley on the other side of the Nile from Thebes. His mummy lay in its coffin until A.D. 1922, when an archaeologist suddenly came across the entrance to his tomb. Most other tombs in the valley had been robbed by thieves but this one was almost untouched. Even though Tutankhamen was not an important pharaoh, superb treasures were discovered in his tomb. Among other objects were a beautiful solid gold face mask (**above**), a gold casket containing his coffin, chairs and beds coated in gold, exquisite jewelry and, being a young king when he died, even his favorite catapult. All these objects were just as they had been when put into the tomb more than three thousand years before.

Nilometer

Nilometers were built at different spots along the river to measure the Nile's rise and fall. The early ones made by the ancient Egyptians were just high and low water marks on cliffs or buildings. This one in Cairo was built in the 9th Century A.D. It is much more accurate than earlier ones and uses tunnels to carry Nile water into a well. The water level is measured on the central column. By keeping records, the Egyptians were able to know in advance if the flood was going to be good or bad each year.

5
Explorers of the Nile

Until the last century, no one knew for sure where the source of the Nile lay. Neither the ancient Egyptians nor the Greeks and Romans who followed them discovered it. Exploring this area was difficult. The river was long and the swamps of the Sudd made a very difficult barrier to pass.

Already by the end of the 1600s. Jesuit priests had come across the source of the Blue Nile. But no one had explored this area properly. In 1768 James Bruce, a rich Scotsman, set off on some hair-raising adventures trying to follow the Blue Nile as it churned through the steep gorges in Ethiopia. Although he reached the source of the Blue Nile, he was not able to explore the river all the way. To this day, no one has managed to travel along the whole length of this wild Nile tributary.

It was almost another hundred years before a real attempt was made to find out where the White Nile rose. The nineteenth century was a great period of exploration and discovery by Europeans in Africa, and many explorers desperately wanted to be the first to find the source of the Nile.

The first famous explorer was an Englishman, Richard Burton; he knew Africa well and spoke many languages. With him went another Englishman, John Hannington Speke. In 1857 they set off from the east coast of Africa, hoping they could reach the Nile south of the Sudd, which had stopped others. Things went wrong almost immediately. Malaria struck; pack animals died; porters abandoned them. After a terrible seven months, suffering from illness and fever, the explorers finally reached the shores of Lake Tanganyika (bordering present-day Zaire and Tanzania), which had never been seen by Europeans before this time.

Ptolemy's Map

In 150 A.D. Ptolemy, a famous Greek geographer made a map showing the source of the Nile as being the Mountains of the Moon. He was only able to guess at the source because no one had explored that far. He drew his map after listening to stories heard by merchants who had traveled upstream. You can see from this copy of his map that he was very close to the truth.

Claudius Ptolemy lived in Alexandria in the second century A.D. His book, *Guide to Geography*, with maps, was used by explorers for many centuries.

The American explorer Henry Stanley finally meets David Livingstone at Ujiji, near Lake Tanganyika. Livingstone had been missing for several years.

Burton fell ill and while he stopped to rest, Speke went on north to explore. He came across a huge lake which he named Lake Victoria. Speke guessed it was the source of the Nile. Burton refused to believe this and argued that Lake Tanganyika was the source.

After he returned home, Speke became famous. He wanted to prove that he had found the true source of the Nile and so, two years later, he set out again on another expedition. As before it was hard going, with pack animals dying and food running low. But Speke managed to reach Lake Victoria and discovered a big river flowing north out of it. Speke was sure that this was the Nile. He returned to London a hero. However, Burton was

Speke and Burton are received at a king's court in central Africa.

determined to prove that the river Speke had found was not the Nile. It was decided to hold a public debate on the matter between the two men. Unfortunately the day before the debate Speke died in a hunting accident. He died never knowing that in fact he was right.

Still the Nile had not yet been properly explored. Others followed Burton and Speke. In 1861, another Englishman, Samuel Baker and his wife Florence, approached the source the difficult way, traveling up the Nile itself. After two years they finally made it through the Sudd, only to be attacked by the local people and stricken by illness. Eventually they reached Lake Albert and the river that flowed into it. The Bakers had mapped yet another stretch of the very large Nile River.

The famous Dr. David Livingstone also played a part in solving the puzzle of the Nile. In 1865 the great Scottish explorer set out to look for the source. He had so many troubles that he lost touch with the outside world for four years and was presumed dead. An American journalist, Henry Stanley, set out to find Livingstone. After nearly a year he reached Lake Tanganyika where he found the doctor alive.

The two men mapped Lake Tanganyika and found that it could not be the source of the Nile. On another later expedition, in 1875, by sailing all the way around Lake Victoria, Stanley was able to prove that the Nile really did begin there and not at another lake. John Speke's discovery was finally proved to be right.

The Slave Trade

Four thousand years ago peoples from the upper Nile were forced into slavery by ancient Egyptians. Carvings on temples show Nubian slaves tied together and transported downriver. Later the Arabs continued this practice. The British and other European countries too took up slavery in Africa as a way of obtaining cheap labor for their new colonies. Millions of Africans were captured and shipped abroad. Although slavery was abolished in the British Empire by the mid-1800s, at least 50,000 slaves were being brought down from the Upper Nile every year. Many of those taken were from the Sudan where 15,000 Arab traders continued to run the huge slavery business.

6
Agriculture and Irrigation

Farming in Egypt

Food and other crops can only be grown in Egypt by using water from the Nile, since hardly any rain falls. Because the weather is usually warm and sunny and there is now a regular flow of water in the river since the building of the Aswan Dam, many different types of crops can be grown all year round.

As well as basic foods like wheat, rice, corn, and vegetables, crops such as sugar, rice, fruits—particularly dates, oranges, and bananas—are grown for sale. Sugar is an increasingly important crop in Egypt and several refineries have been built along the Nile. Cotton grows especially well in Egypt and much is exported abroad. All over Egypt, too, are rich green fields of *berseem,* a kind of clover grown as animal feed. From the river come fish like the Nile perch.

Tractors like this one being used beside the Nile are too expensive for most Egyptian farmers. Many still use donkeys, mules, or water buffalo to do the heavy work.

Egyptian farmers are called *fellahin.* Most own their own land and farm it themselves. Usually they grow what they need to live on plus another crop to sell for cash. Life is hard for many and they have few luxuries. As well as a donkey or water buffalo, which is used to do work such as plowing the fields or carrying loads, farmers might raise chickens and often keep pigeons to eat.

The Nile Delta is the most densely farmed area—every square inch of land is used. However, around some towns good farmland is disappearing because the land is more valuable for building houses.

Irrigation

Even though the river has water, it is ineffective unless the water is controlled and taken to the fields. Over thousands of years the people of the Nile have developed methods to irrigate their land. The annual flooding of the Nile before the Aswan Dam was built was vital for irrigation. Directed by barrages, the high flood water was drawn off into basins, left to settle, and then the damp rich soil was planted with crops.

Now the Aswan Dam has controlled the floods themselves and regulated the water so that it flows evenly during the

Opposite These men are harvesting dates in the Nile Delta. The man has climbed the tree to cut down the bunches of dates, which are lowered to the ground in a basket.

Below Sugarcane is an important crop in Egypt. Here it is being brought to a central collection point by donkeys, which are often used to bring the crops in from the fields.

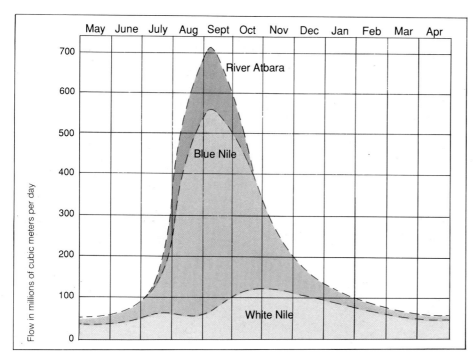

Three main tributaries bring water into the Nile—the Blue Nile, the White Nile, and the Atbara River. Barrages and dams help to store water and release it when the rivers are low. This graph shows the different levels of the Nile and its tributaries at different times of the year.

The *shadoof* is an ancient method of watering the fields that is still used today.

year. In order to bring water from the Nile close to the fields, long canals have been built, some stretching many miles. The water that flows into these canals is regulated by big barrages that have been built across the Nile in many places. These have gates that can be opened and shut and thereby carefully control where the water goes.

Irrigation methods used by the farmers in bringing the water from the canals to their fields are hundreds of years old. The weighted *shadoof* balances a bucket of water as it is raised to the field. Animals turn a wheel called a *sakia* that scoops water up and onto the fields. A long tube called an Archimedes' screw pulls up water as a handle is turned. Although many farmers now use a diesel-fueled pump that is far quicker, these old irrigation methods are still used all along the Nile in Egypt.

Over the last few years, Egypt has greatly increased its agricultural production. However, it is not enough to feed the large and growing population. Wheat has to be imported every year.

The government would like to bring more land into agricultural use. There are several plans that all involve using Nile water and piping it to areas which at the moment are useless desert. Projects like this have already started in Khārga Oasis and in the desert areas on the fringe of the Nile delta. A huge project is also planned to develop 617,500 acres on either side of the Suez Canal—using water from the Nile.

All of these plans depend on whether there will be enough water in the Nile. Currently Egypt uses all the water that it is allowed under an agreement with the Sudan; some of the big irrigation projects have already been given up because of lack of water. In the future there may be conflicts between the countries that lie beside the river over who can use the water.

Farther up the Nile, the Sudan has its own irrigation projects such as Gezira between the Blue and White Niles south of Khartoum. To the south, in the swamps of the Sudd, a huge canal is being built. The Jonglei Canal will drain part of the Sudd to stop so much water from being lost by evaporation so that more is available for irrigation downstream. The civil war in Sudan has halted work on this for the moment.

Basin Irrigation

Before the Aswan Dam was built the farming year was controlled by the Nile. In about July the river would begin to rise and by September the land would be flooded. Water was directed as far as possible into basins separated by embankments and left to settle. Farmer had little to do until November when the flood water had drained away. Then the planting season would begin. The third season would be the harvest, usually in May. The land would then rest and be refreshed by the Nile flood waters.

The Gezira Project

Gezira is a huge irrigated area between the Blue and the White Nile in Sudan. The region has low rainfall but, by damming the Blue Nile first at Sennar and later at Roseires, stored water has been channeled along a network of canals to irrigate the land.

Originally about 296,400 acres, the project has been extended south to about 2,223,000 acres. As well as the plentiful water, the fine black soil brought down by the Nile has helped crops to grow successfully. The most important crop is cotton which is Sudan's main export. In Kenana, the southern part of the Gezira region, there is a huge sugarcane estate and beef cattle are raised there. Gezira produces much of the country's food, although much more could be grown instead of cash crops (like cotton) to help feed the many hungry people of the Sudan.

A fisher in the Nile Delta has an empty net. Today there are fewer fish to catch.

Many people in the Sudan are nomads, moving from place to place with their cattle to find water and pasture.

Farming in the Upper Nile

Methods of farming are very different along the upper reaches of the Nile. Many of the tribes of southern Sudan live by raising cattle and fishing, leading a nomadic life, dependent on the seasons. The wet season brings good grazing for the cattle on the plains; the dry season often means migrating to the Sudd, where the swamps dry out a little and the cattle can feed. Traditionally, few farm crops are grown though this is changing as the Sudanese government tries to settle the people.

In the far south of the Upper Nile region, in Uganda, there is enough regular rain for crops to be grown anywhere. As well as many vegetables and fruits, coffee, tea, and cotton are produced in Uganda. The great lakes like Lake Victoria and Lake Albert are full of fish and many of those who live by the lake shores fish for a living.

7
Cities, Industry, and Transportation

Cairo

Cairo is not only the biggest city on the Nile, it is also the largest city in Africa. Its population is about fifteen million, including the suburbs. The city is polluted and chaotic, full of noise and traffic. The old ways and the modern ways and the East and the West meet as gleaming office buildings tower over carts pulled by donkeys trotting through the streets below.

Modern Cairo is the center of government, industry, and education in Egypt and is home to nearly one quarter of the Egyptian population. The old part of the city has a maze of narrow streets and busy markets. Tea and coffee houses spill out onto the alleyways and men sit smoking waterpipes.

Four cities have been built at this point on the Nile over the centuries, but none as large as present-day Cairo. Today the city sprawls into the desert

Cairo is the largest city in Africa. It is a noisy, busy city with pollution from both traffic and the sand and dust that blow from the surrounding desert.

The Khan el Khalili market in Cairo is very large, with many shops and stalls and winding narrow alleyways.

beyond the green Nile Valley. Along with rows of new apartment buildings, large industrial suburbs spread out in all directions. There are steel mills, cement and chemical factories, and food and cotton processing plants. Cotton grown in Egypt is world famous.

Cairo is well-known for its film industry which produces films for other Arabic-speaking countries. The city also probably holds the record for the oldest tourist industry in the world. Even in 450 B.C. Greek travelers came to visit the pyramids that lie in the desert on the edge of Cairo. Today, because the ancient Egyptian tombs and temples are so well preserved, millions of tourists flock to Egypt every year. Tourism is the most important means of earning foreign money for Egypt after oil.

The Delta cities

Alexandria, like Cairo, has a long and varied history. It is on the Mediterranean coast and was named Alexandria after the Greek invader, Alexander the Great, who conquered Egypt in 332 B.C. For several hundred years Alexandria was the center of the Western world. No other city could match its huge library containing more than five hundred thousand works. Its massive lighthouse, over 425 feet high, was considered one of the great wonders of the world (it was later destroyed by an earthquake). Cleopatra, the last Egyptian queen and ruler of Alexandria, killed herself so that she would not be captured by the invading Roman army and be exhibited in victory in Rome.

Mohammed, a Caleche Driver

"I drive a horse-drawn carriage called a *caleche* in the town of Luxor. I sit up in the front and my passengers sit behind me with a hood over their seats. Early in the morning I take children to school and later I drive tourists around the sights. Luxor is full of ancient temples and tombs and nearly everyone who lives here does some work connected with the tourist industry."

Today Alexandria has become a modern industrial center of about four million people. It is also a popular seaside resort for Egyptians. Alexandria is the largest city on the Nile delta and Egypt's main port, handling more than eighty percent of Egypt's imports and exports. Marsh land in the delta is being drained to provide more building land and factories are spreading out westward into the desert.

Port Said, a much newer city, was built in 1859 at the northern (Mediterranean) end of the Suez Canal. In the days when the Suez Canal was the main transport route from Europe to Asia, Port Said was a thriving trading center. Today the Egyptian government is encouraging new industry there. Suez, on the Red Sea at the other end of the canal, is a growing town too, with oil refineries processing oil from the Red Sea.

The Suez Canal cuts the distance for ships sailing to the Far East. Here it is shown at Port Said.

Abu, a Nubian Boat Worker

"I am a Nubian from Aswan and I sail a traditional Egyptian Nile boat called a *felucca*. I have been taking tourists up and down the Nile for twenty-five years. Often I show them the Nubian villages on the banks of the Nile. Our villages here haven't changed much but many Nubian people live in new towns. They were moved from their homes beside the Nile when the Aswan Dam was built. Lake Nasser flooded huge areas by the Nile where Nubians lived."

Khartoum

Lying where the Blue and White Niles meet, Khartoum is the capital of the Sudan. Its name means elephant trunk—which is the shape of the land just before the two rivers meet. The modern city of Khartoum was laid out in the shape of a Union Jack by the British. The British took control of Khartoum in 1898, after the defeat of the Mahdi, a fanatical Sudanese religious leader. After besieging Khartoum, the Mahdi's warriors had hacked to death a British army officer, General Gordon.

Farming is the main way of living for most Sudanese, so most industry is based on agriculture. Factories in Khartoum process food and produce textiles, leather, and cotton; the Sudan exports peanuts, sugar, and cotton. A major project in the Sudan was the building of a massive sugar refinery at Kosti, 185 miles south of Khartoum.

Opposite For centuries camels have been used for transportation in the Nile Valley and the desert.
Below A rooftop view of the city of Khartoum shows modern buildings and mosques.

Feluccas, the traditional Nile sailing boats, are now mainly used by tourists.

Transportation on the Nile

Since ancient times people not only used the Nile to water their crops but also to transport themselves and their goods between one place and another. Boats were made from wood or papyrus reeds and powered with sails or oars. The winds would help blow the boat upstream and the current would move the boat downstream.

The Nile has never been an easy river to navigate because the many cataracts stopped boats from sailing all the way up. The Sudd was also a barrier for many boats. Even when a channel was cleared, vegetation would often grow over again very quickly. Apart from the great lakes, much of the upper part of the Nile was impassable because of the strong rapids.

In the colonial days of the nineteenth century, the British brought in steam boats to speed up transportation. Now roads, railroads, and airplanes have taken the place of boats because they provide faster ways of traveling. Egypt's roads and railroads are fairly good but Sudan has been unable to keep its transportation system in good condition. Traveling in that country is very slow.

The traditional wooden sailing boats, called *feluccas*, still exist on the Nile but today they are mostly used by tourists. Luxury liners now crowd sections of the Nile, taking visitors to see the famous temples. Apart from fishers, local people only regularly use boats in the Sudd and on the lakes. The traditional means of transportation for short journeys beside the river, and still used by many farmers today, is the donkey or camel.

8
Famine and Refugees

As long as the Nile has water, people who live nearby can grow food to eat. But away from the river, water supplies are much less reliable. In Ethiopia and th southern part of the Sudan there is seasonal rainfall. If the rains do not come, droughts can cause hunger and even starvation.

In the early 1980s drought hit many parts of central and northern Africa.

Millions of people starved and died. In Ethiopia farmers could no longer grow crops or keep livestock. They sold all they had to buy food. That soon ran out and they left their farms to search for food and water. More than one million people fled from Ethiopia, many going to the Sudan. But the Sudan too was hit by drought and more than two million Sudanese were also on the move.

These withered stalks are all that is left of crops planted in a region affected by drought in the Sudan.

Many young Ethiopian refugees have lost their parents through war and famine.

The drought itself would not have been such a disaster if it had not been for civil war in both the Sudan and Ethiopia. The governments could not or would not provide help for their hungry people. The fighting caused many to flee their homes, and others already strug-

Wheat arrives from Canada to help feed starving people in Ethiopia.

gling to feed themselves had to cope with huge numbers of refugees.

Foreign aid slowly came to the area. Refugee camps were set up in the east of the Sudan where there was no fighting. People were arriving so fast that one camp grew from 5,000 to 35,000 people in a few days. Many died from weakness before they could reach the camps.

Relief and charity organizations tried to provide water, food, and medical help. Water was in short supply, which meant that people could not wash regularly and diseases spread rapidly. People lined up for small rations of food and others just sat listlessly waiting for death.

Feeding and helping refugees in the Sudan and Ethiopia is difficult. The roads in these areas are very bad, so getting transportation and gasoline to take relief supplies is a problem. Convoys are often attacked if they pass through a war zone and trucks may be captured for use in the war, so food and medical supplies often never arrive at the refugee camps.

Camps remain in the east of the Sudan and Ethiopia, housing approximately half a million refugees. Civil war in the Sudan and fighting in Ethiopia continue to make it difficult for people to return to their homes. Although the rains came again for a year or two in the late 1980s, drought is striking again—this time across the whole of Africa. The scale of the disaster in the 1990s could be far worse than in 1983 and 1984.

The problems of drought and war are made worse by the years of bad agricultural policies and misuse of the soil. People tend to overuse the poor soils, which need a rest between crops to re-

A tented refugee camp for thousands fleeing from civil war in the Sudan provides help.

gain nutrients. Fertilizers are too expensive for most poor farmers. The cattle herders have overgrazed their lands; often they have been prevented from moving their animals to new grazing because of war or for other reasons such as irrigation or agricultural projects. Trees that hold moisture in the soil and keep it from being washed away have been cut down, causing the land to become even more barren.

The governments of the Sudan and Ethiopia have tried growing cash crops (like cotton, sugar, and coffee) that can be sold abroad. These crops are grown on the best land and the ordinary farmers are left with poor land on which to grow food to live. In the Sudan, sorghum and corn production has fallen by more than half, even though they are the basic foodstuffs for the local people. The population continues to grow.

Foreign aid to help these countries is provided in two ways. One is emergency aid (sending food and medical help) when there is a crisis. The other is long-term aid. Many aid organizations try to help by sending experts to advise on projects such as tree planting, irrigation systems, and the best crops to grow.

A relief organization poster draws attention to the plight of the starving people of Africa.

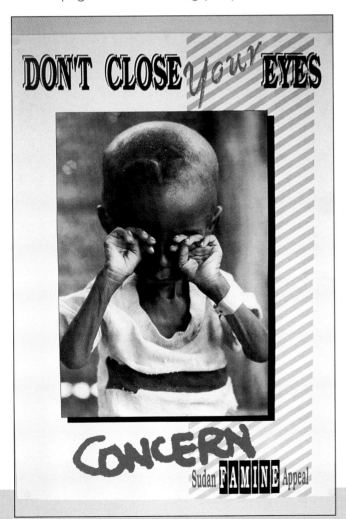

DON'T CLOSE *your* EYES

CONCERN

Sudan FAMINE Appeal

39

In a small though successful way people managed to control the flow of water in the Nile for nearly five thousand years. However, big floods sometimes caused terrible destruction in the Lower Nile valley and at other times there would be too little water. Relying on the Nile's annual flood for irrigation was very risky. It also meant that only one crop a year could be grown.

In the nineteenth century it was thought that a solution to this problem was found. By building dams along the river, flood water could be held back and stored in reservoirs, and let out whenever it was needed. This would give a steady flow all year round without the seasonal changes. And so the first dam at Aswan in Egypt was built in 1902.

Controlling the water

The dam partly controlled the flow of water but it was found to be too small. Egypt's population was growing rapidly and more flood-free and irrigated land was needed for food. So a grand plan was prepared for what was then one of the biggest dams in the world. It was begun in 1960, 4 miles upstream from the old dam. A huge channel was cut in the rock beside the Nile and the excavated material was used as a base for the new dam. When the dam was finished, the Nile water was forced to flow through this diversion channel where it was used to create hydroelectricity.

The Aswan Dam was said to be modern Egypt's "pyramid"—except it was

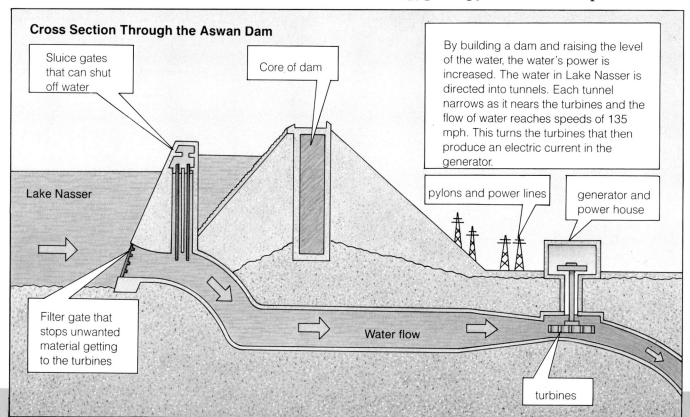

Cross Section Through the Aswan Dam

Sluice gates that can shut off water

Core of dam

By building a dam and raising the level of the water, the water's power is increased. The water in Lake Nasser is directed into tunnels. Each tunnel narrows as it nears the turbines and the flow of water reaches speeds of 135 mph. This turns the turbines that then produce an electric current in the generator.

Lake Nasser

pylons and power lines

generator and power house

Filter gate that stops unwanted material getting to the turbines

Water flow

turbines

Sayeed, a Worker at the Aswan Dam

"Behind me is the great Aswan Dam. I work here at the hydroelectricity station. Water from Lake Nasser pours through six great tunnels and drops 100 feet with great force. This power is used to turn turbines which make the electricity. Aswan has become a big town and we have a huge fertilizer factory that runs on electricity from the dam. There are many chemical and fertilizer factories now in Egypt because the Nile no longer floods and fertilizes the valley naturally every year."

seventeen times larger than the biggest pyramid. In 1970 the 2-mile-long dam was finished. Gradually a huge lake, Lake Nasser (named after Egypt's former president), formed behind the dam, covering an enormous area, 3,720 square miles.

The dam has meant that farmers in the Lower Nile valley now have a regular supply of water. As a result crops are

A huge barrage crosses the Nile just north of Cairo. The water is controlled so that it a can be fed into canals for irrigation in the Nile Delta.

grown all year round, the amount of farmland that can be used has expanded by thirty percent, and Egypt has greatly increased its food production. During the terrible droughts of the 1980s, by storing water in this way, Egypt was spared the suffering that hit the Sudan and Ethiopia.

The Aswan Dam has not only controlled the annual floods in Egypt but also provided electricity for the whole country. Hydroelectricity has the advantage that it is a renewable and nonpolluting source of energy.

However, despite these advantages, the costs have been high. When the dam was built and Lake Nasser began to fill, thousands of Nubian people were forced to leave their homes. They were moved to new towns and villages. Their way of life has been totally changed; some have managed to cope while others are very unhappy at losing their traditional homelands.

The rising waters of Lake Nasser also began to cover ancient Egyptian temples and buildings that had been built along the banks of the Nile above Aswan. A few of these temples were moved, stone by stone, at enormous cost, to new sites but several still lie today under Lake Nasser.

Abu Simbel Temple

This great temple was built to honor the Egyptian pharaoh Ramses II nearly 3,000 years ago. It almost disappeared under the waters of Lake Nasser as it filled behind the Aswan Dam. A great rescue operation was put together by UNESCO in 1964. First, the temple was cut up into huge blocks of stone. Then a mountain was especially built on land above the level of the lake. Finally, the temple and all of its statues were moved and reconstructed in their new home.

Problems for the future

Downstream there have been some damaging results from the dam. The annual floods no longer bring the rich fertile silt downstream; it is being held back by the dam. Instead, farmers have to use expensive chemical fertilizers to feed their fields with nutrients. The nutrients in the silt also once fed fish; now there are far less fish, both in the Nile River and in the waters off the coast.

Because so much more water is being used in irrigation, the general level of water in the earth, called the water table, has risen. As it has risen, it has brought up salts which usually lie lower down in the soil. These salts make the land infertile, so that crops cannot be grown. Any salts in the soil in the past were flushed out by the floods. Now about one-third of Egypt's irrigated land is affected by salt that is impossible to remove. Much of the irrigated land has become waterlogged, too. When the water evaporates even more salts are deposited.

These problems are found everywhere Nile waters are being used for irrigation. Good soil drainage is needed to stop

A farmer puts fertilizer on his fields. The Aswan Dam has stopped the floods that once brought down fertile silt every year.

The rising level of the water table is bringing salts to the surface. This field is becoming infertile because of white salt.

this from happening, but drains are very expensive to put in all the fields.

The building of a huge number of irrigation canals has also led to increased disease. Both malarial mosquitoes and bilharzia parasites thrive in still water. Still water, in dam reservoirs, behind barrages, and in canals, has also encouraged the water hyacinth. This plant grows so fast that it can cover a canal in a few weeks and it quickly clogs up waterways. Herbicides are used to remove it, but they pollute the water. To remove the plant by machine takes a great deal of time.

Although the reservoir means that there is a regular water supply, massive amounts of water are lost. Billions of cubic feet evaporate every year from Lake Nasser—enough to irrigate nearly two and a half million acres of farmland. The life of the dam itself is in question because all the silt which previously flowed into Egypt is now being deposited by the Nile in Lake Nasser. It will take some time but eventually the lake will completely fill with silt and the Aswan Dam will be useless. Other dams built on the Nile and its tributaries face the same problems. There is also another danger for the dam. If it were to collapse or be destroyed by war or an act of terrorism, virtually the whole of Egypt could be destroyed.

Millions of people depend on the Nile for their life. Modern controls like dams do not solve all the problems; maybe we should look at the traditional methods of water control and irrigation to help us find better long-term solutions.

Opposite A tourist boat steams along the river bordered by green and fertile fields. Just beyond the valley lies the barren and hostile desert.

Below Thick rafts of water hyacinth build up against barrages on the Nile, blocking the river.

Glossary

Archaeologist Someone who studies ancient buildings and objects.

Bantu A member of the indigenous (native) peoples living in central, eastern, and southern Africa.

Barrages Human-made barriers used across rivers to control the water's speed and flow; usually there are gates in the barrage that can be lifted up to let water through.

Barren Unable to grow anything.

Bilharzia parasite Types of worm that live in snails in the water and cause a disease that can make people very ill.

Cataracts Waterfalls or rapids where the river spills over rocks.

Colonized To be ruled or governed by people from another country.

Convoys Several trucks traveling together, often with an army escort.

Delta A flat fan-shaped area where a river splits into channels at the end of its course.

Depression A hollow or area lower than the surrounding land.

Droughts Long periods with little or no rain.

Embalmed A way of preserving a dead body by removing the insides and drying the body out with salt.

Embankments Banks specially built to contain water.

Eroded Worn away by weather or water.

Evaporation Loss of water into the air when it is warmed up.

Excavated Scooped out or dug out.

Extinction Dying out completely.

Famine A severe shortage of food when many people do not have enough to eat.

Fertile Able to make things grow well.

Flood plain The flat land beside rivers where they regularly flood and deposit sediment.

Herbicides Chemicals used to kill weeds.

Hydroelectricity Electricity made from the power of falling water.

Islam The religion of Muslims, followers of the teachings of the Prophet Muhammad.

Jesuit A Roman Catholic missionary.

Malaria An illness caused by the bite of certain kinds of mosquitoes.

Middle East An area including the Arabic-speaking countries around the eastern end of the Mediterranean Sea.

Migrating Moving from one place to settle in another.

Mummy A preserved dead body.

Nomadic Not living in a fixed place but wandering from place to place.

Nutrients Minerals that plants (or animals) need to help them grow.

Oases Fertile places in the desert.

Papyrus A tall reedy plant, once common in Egypt and once used to make paper.

Rapids Fast-flowing part of a river; often there are rocks sticking out of the riverbed.

Refineries Factories where raw materials, such as sugar and oil, are cleaned and purified.

Renewable Able to be replaced or replenished.

Reservoir A human-made lake in which water is stored.

Sediment Material like clay, sand, or stones carried by a river and then deposited.

Silt Very fine particles of soil and rock carried by a river.

Spits Long narrow reefs of land running into the sea.

Suez Canal A canal built between the Mediterranean Sea and the Red Sea. It was completed in 1869 and it shortened the length of time taken by ships sailing between India and Europe; they no longer had to sail around Africa.

Tributaries Rivers that run into other rivers.

Waterlogged So much water in the soil that it becomes unfit to use.

UNESCO The United Nations Educational, Scientific, and Cultural Organization.

Upper Nile Commonly used to describe the area upstream of the Aswan Dam and Lake Nasser.

BOOKS TO READ AND USEFUL ADDRESSES

Books to Read

Ancient Egypt by Charles Alexander Robinson (Franklin Watts, 1984)

Discovering Tut-ankh Amen's Tomb by Shirley Glubok (Macmillan Publishing Co., 1968)

Egypt (Enchantment of the World) by Wilbur Cross (Childrens Press, 1982)

The Egyptians (The Ancient World) by Pamela Odijk (Silver Burdett Press, 1989)

Inside Story: An Egyptian Pyramid by Jacqueline Morley (Simon & Schuster, 1991)

Issues: Famine in Africa by Lloyd Timberlake (Franklin Watts, 1990)

The Nile (Rivers of the World) by E. Barton Worthington (Silver Burdett, 1978)

The Pharaohs of Ancient Egypt by Elizabeth Payne (Random House, 1964)

The Pyramid Builders (Turning Points in World History) by Carter Smith III (Silver Burdett Press, 1991)

What do we know about the Egyptians? by Joanna Defrates (Simon & Schuster, 1991)

Useful Addresses

The Metropolitan Museum of Art
Fifth Avenue at 82nd Street
New York, NY 10028
(contains the complete Temple of Dendur, an early Christian sculpture from Egypt)

Egyptian Tourist Authority
323 Geray Street
San Francisco, CA 94102

Cairo Museum
Cairo
Egypt

The following organizations will supply pamphlets and information about famine relief in the countries of the Upper Nile.

Save The Children
54 Wilton Road
Westport, CT 06880

UNICEF
333 East 38th Street
New York, NY 10016

Picture acknowledgments

All photographs including the cover by Julia Waterlow except the following: Concern 39 (lower); © Michael Holford 17; Hutchison Library 8 (top), 10, Sarah Errington 37; Mansell Collection 23 (top), 24; Topham Picture Library 38 (both), 39 (top); Tropix D. Davis 16 (lower), 30, 34 (lower), R. Cansdale 8, J. Schmid 6. The map on page 5 is by Peter Bull Design. Artwork on pages 9, 28, and 40 is by John Yates.

INDEX

Numbers in **bold** refer to illustrations